Machine Identity Protection

Venafi Special Edition

A Wiley Brand

Machine Identity Protection For Dummies®, Venafi Special Edition

Published by
John Wiley & Sons, Inc.
111 River St.
Hoboken, NJ 07030-5774
www.wiley.com

For general information on our other products and services, or how to create a custom *For Dummies* book for your business or organization, please contact our Business Development Department in the U.S. at 877-409-4177, contact info@dummies.biz, or visit www.wiley.com/go/custompub. For information about licensing the *For Dummies* brand for products or services, contact BrandedRights&Licenses@Wiley.com.

ISBN: 978-1-119-49131-6 (pbk); ISBN: 978-1-119-49130-9 (ebk)

Manufactured in the United States of America

C10004528_092018

Publisher's Acknowledgments

Some of the people who helped bring this book to market include the following:

Project Editor: Carrie A. Burchfield

Editorial Manager: Rev Mengle

Acquisitions Editor: Amy Fandrei

Business Development Representative: Karen Hattan

Table of Contents

Introduction

D id you know that businesses spend billions each year on identity and access management? But almost all of this money is spent on protecting the digital identities of humans — usernames and passwords. Businesses spend almost nothing on protecting machine identities, even though our entire digital economy hinges on secure communications between machines.

About This Book

Welcome to *Machine Identity Protection For Dummies*, Venafi Special Edition. This book helps you understand where machine identities are used in your network and what you need to do to keep these identities up-to-date and protected. You discover how machine identities contribute to your encryption strategy and what you need to do to protect the growing number of machine identities that your infrastructure requires. After reading this book, you'll know why you should make protecting machine identities a priority in your organization.

Feel free to explore the information contained in this book as you wish; go to any part that interests you immediately, or read it from cover to cover. We wrote this book with a sequential logic, but if you want to jump to a specific topic, you can start anywhere to extract good stuff!

Foolish Assumptions

In writing this book, we knew that the information would be useful to many people, but we have to admit that we made a few assumptions about who we think you are. We assume that

>> You want to learn more about the weakest areas of your organization's security program.

>> You're a Public Key Infrastructure (PKI) administrator or a system administrator responsible for properly managing your organization's encryption assets. Or, you manage this function within your organization's security or operations group.

>> You're somewhat familiar with encryption and security.

>> You want to discover the easiest, most effective, and direct way to protect your machine identities.

Icons Used in This Book

We occasionally use special icons to focus attention on important items. Here's what you'll find in this book:

REMEMBER

The Remember icon highlights important facts about machine identities and their protection. So sip your coffee and read on.

TIP

The Tip icon gives you the best ways to lower machine identity risks. This content helps you get the most out of your protection efforts.

WARNING

The Warning icon flags risky situations that, if not dealt with, can leave your organization more vulnerable to cybercriminal attacks. So take note! The information in this section can help you prioritize your machine identity protection program tasks.

TECHNICAL STUFF

The Technical Stuff icon notes when the book goes a little deeper into the nitty gritty of machine identity protection. You don't need this information to understand the rest of the book, but this gives the techie types more details.

Beyond the Book

Want to learn more about your organization's machine identity exposure? You can sign up for a free certificate risk assessment at `www.venafi.com/risk-assessment`.

Chapter **1**

Understanding Machine Identities and Why They Need Protection

Machines are driving unprecedented improvements in business efficiency, productivity, agility, and speed. But machines don't work in isolation. They need to be in constant communication with other machines. Before machines can communicate securely, they need some way to determine if the other machine is trustworthy.

When online, humans rely on usernames and passwords to iden-tify and authenticate themselves to machines. Machines also have digital identities, but they don't rely on usernames and passwords for authentication. Instead, they rely on cryptographic keys and digital certificates that serve as machine identities.

At the beginning of every secure communication, machines check these digital identities to establish trust, authenticate other machines, and encrypt communication. In this chapter, you dis-cover how machines are used to enable all kinds of digital com-munications and how these machine identities work — and you also see why they need to be protected.

Understanding How Machine Identities Are Used

Machines use encrypted connections to establish trust in all kinds of digital transactions. To do this, machines identities use digital certificates and cryptographic keys (discussed later in this chapter in the section "Defining Machine Identities") to validate the legitimacy of both communicating machines. To better understand how this works, we give you some of the ways machine identities are used to support vital business functions:

>> **Securing web transactions with HTTPS:** Digital certificates, such as Secure Sockets Layer (SSL) or Transport Layer Security (TLS) certificates, are critical to the security of web transactions, such as online banking and e-commerce. These certificates enable an encrypted connection between a web browser and web server.

WARNING

If the certificates used to secure HTTPS aren't protected, cybercriminals can gain access to these critical machine identities. Once this happens, cybercriminals can eavesdrop on encrypted traffic or impersonate a trusted system.

>> **Securing privileged access:** Secure Shell (SSH) is often used to secure system-administrator-to-machine access for routine tasks. SSH is also used to secure the machine-to-machine automation of critical business functions, such as automatically triggering operations and routine file transfers. SSH keys ensure that only trusted users and machines have access to sensitive network systems and data.

WARNING

Cybercriminals misappropriate poorly protected SSH keys to bypass security controls and gain privileged access to internal network resources and data. With SSH keys, attackers can appear to be legitimate administrators or trusted machines, enabling them to hide and move around on internal networks, often for extended periods of time without being detected.

>> **Securing Fast IT and DevOps:** Development Operations (DevOps) teams are focused on speeding up the delivery of products and services. To do this, developers use cloud-based, self-contained runtime environments, known as *containers,* to run individual modules called *microservices.*

Each microservice and container should have a certificate to identify and authenticate it and to support encryption. These certificates serve as valid machine identities that allow containers to communicate securely with other containers, microservices, the cloud, and the Internet.

WARNING

In the fast-paced world of DevOps, issuing keys and certificates manually can slow the delivery of IT services. The resulting frustration can cause developers to avoid encryption altogether, take shortcuts with SSH keys, or to otherwise skimp on key and certificate security. When this happens, it exposes your organization to unnecessary security vulnerabilities, and it can also insert error-prone, manual steps into an increasingly automated DevOps environment.

>> **Securing communication on consumer devices:** With increasing numbers of remote and mobile workers, enterprises are using Mobile Device Management (MDM) and Enterprise Mobility Management (EMM) to balance enterprise security with bring-your-own-device (BYOD) practices. Digital certificates are a vital element of mobile security; they provide the foundation for authenticating mobile devices that access enterprise networks. Also, mobile device certificates are increasingly being used to enable access to enterprise Wi-Fi networks and for remote enterprise access using SSL and IPSEC VPNs. In addition, mobile access to Internet of Things (IoT) devices on enterprise networks relies on certificates for authentication.

WARNING

Mobile security (MDM/EMM) and keys and certificates are frequently managed by different teams with different objectives. Without central oversight, consistent machine identity security and protection for mobile devices is nearly impossible. Two very common examples of inconsistent mobile machine identity security are the use of a duplicated certificate on multiple devices and the on-going use of unrevoked certificates issued to past employees. Both are poor practices that allow mobile certificates to be misused.

>> **Authenticating software code:** Software is usually signed with a certificate to verify the integrity of the software. Users implicitly trust products when they are signed by a reliable publisher's code-signing certificates, believing that the signed software is safe to deploy. When used properly, these certificates serve as a machine identity that authenticates the software.

It is very lucrative for cybercriminals to steal poorly protected code-signing certificates from legitimate companies and use them to sign malicious code. When the malicious code is signed with a stolen, legitimate certificate, it doesn't trigger any warnings, and unsuspecting users will mistakenly trust that the malicious code is safe to install and use.

Defining Machine Identities

To understand how to protect machine identities, you need to know a little more about the security assets that make up machine identities: cryptographic keys and digital certificates.

Cryptographic keys

Public key cryptography (or *asymmetric cryptography*) is used to secure machine communications. Matched pairs of asymmetric numbers are used as "keys" (one public and one private) that authenticate, encrypt, and decrypt a digital exchange. These key pairs are used when a machine or person initiates secure, private communications.

A public key can be given to anyone, but the private key must be kept secret by its owner. Public keys can be used by any party that receives them to encrypt data and validate digital signatures. Private keys are only used by their owners to decrypt information (which was encrypted with the public key) or to digitally sign information to prove that it came from the owner of the private key.

Public key cryptography relies on key length and cryptographic algorithms for security. Key length is the length of a key in bits — it's similar to the number of characters in a password. The cryptographic algorithm is the group of mathematical equations used to securely generate and apply key pairs for authentication, encryption, and decryption. Because public key cryptography serves as the basis for secure communications on the Internet, and because most organizations don't protect these critical security assets very well, cybercriminals devote a lot of effort to trying to compromise keys and certificates.

Digital certificates

Whenever you want to communicate securely with another party online, you must make sure you're using that party's public key. To do this, you use a *digital certificate* to associate the public key with its owner. The owner is usually a machine (the definition of machine here is pretty elastic and can include software or a domain such as a website) or, less commonly, a person. A *digital certificate* is also called a *public key certificate.* The majority of certificates used today are based on the international standard X.509.

People rely on X.509 digital certificates because they're issued by a trusted source, called a Certificate Authority (CA), and include several types of identifying information:

>> A public key

>> A unique name for the machine (for example, www. company.com) or the person who owns the certificate

>> The name of the organization that issued the certificate (the issuing CA)

>> An issue date and expiration date, after which the certificate should no longer be used

>> The CA's digital signature

In addition to this information, every certificate includes information about how it should be used. Together, the information in a certificate serves as a machine identity. This identity is checked before a machine can access servers or other machines.

Here's a basic example of how machine identities are used every day: When you attempt to connect to a website from your phone or laptop, the web server provides its machine identity (digital certificate) so you can be sure you're connecting to the correct site. This verification is particularly important if you're going to complete an online transaction, such as making a purchase or completing a banking transaction. Of course, this step is just one in a complex string of machine-to-machine communications needed to complete the transaction. Each subsequent step also requires the machines involved to be identified and authenticated, but this example helps illustrate why protecting machine identities is vital to the security of almost every form of digital communication.

Chapter 2
Recognizing Machine Identity Risks

From service outages to security breaches, weak machine identities can wreak havoc with your business. In this chapter, you look at five of the most common machine identity protection risks and explore how these can impact your business.

Certificate-related Outages

When certificates are issued, they're assigned an expiration date. If a certificate isn't replaced before it expires, it can trigger a certificate-related outage of the system it supports. That unplanned outage and the associated downtime will continue until a new certificate is issued and installed. Without the correct intelligence, such as knowing where a certificate is installed and who owns that system, certificate-related outages are notoriously difficult to diagnose.

WARNING

If a certificate is used on more than one system, such as on load balancers, its expiration can cause simultaneous outages on multiple systems. The consequences of certificate-related outages on critical infrastructure are often so severe that they're the catalyst that forces organizations to re-evaluate the way they manage and secure machine identities.

Security Breaches

Most security controls trust digital communications that are authenticated using machine identities. But when the private keys and certificates that serve as machine identities (we talk about these in Chapter 1) are compromised or forged, cybercriminals can use them to appear legitimate, allowing them to circumvent security controls. Cybercriminals also use stolen machine identities to gain privileged access to critical systems so they can move deeper into your network and stay hidden for extended periods of time.

In addition, cybercriminals know that most enterprise security controls blindly trust encrypted traffic, so they use encryption — such as HTTPS connections — to hide attacks, evade detection, and bypass critical security controls. This is one key reason why most network attacks use HTTPS.

WARNING

Although the details of most breaches aren't made public, many of the largest data breaches exhibit key symptoms of attacks that leverage machine identities, such as abuse of privileged access, pivoting between systems via trusted access, and persistence for long periods of time on the network.

Slow Incident Response

To remain agile enough to avoid the impacts of outages and the increasing number of threats to your machine identities, you must be prepared to respond quickly when needed. For example, what would you do if one of your Certificate Authorities (CAs) was compromised and you needed to replace all the certificates from that CA quickly? Other large-scale security events that require timely response include the discovery of a machine identity using a vulnerable algorithm (for example, SHA-1), the exploit of a cryptographic library bug (one of the most notable was Heartbleed), or when a leading browser decides it will no longer trust certificates issued by one of your CAs.

When you need to respond to any type of event that affects machine identities, time is critical. The longer a security threat, outage, or breach continues, the greater the potential for serious damage.

Operational Inefficiencies

Organizations typically spend an average of four hours per year managing each digital certificate that serves as a machine identity. With thousands, or even hundreds of thousands, of machine identities, the resulting overhead can add up quickly. And if your machine identity operations aren't running smoothly — which is the case in most organizations — the time required can escalate fast, especially when there's an outage or breach.

As more IT workloads move to the cloud, and as more IT services are containerized, manual machine identity creation and management simply can't keep up. In most cases, your system administrators configure and manage machine identities for the systems they control. This makes it very hard to consistently enforce security policies companywide and gather information rapidly when you're trying to respond to a security event.

When you add in other organizational factors, such as administrators who are unfamiliar with certificates or trust stores (where certificates from trusted CAs should be kept), it's easy to see why organizations aren't able to respond quickly to security events that impact or misuse machine identities.

Negative Audit Findings

Machine identities are increasingly subject to corporate, government, and industry policies and regulations, including several standards that focus specifically on cryptographic key and certificate management and security. Because most organizations don't have a strong machine identity protection program, it's not unusual for auditors to discover that an organization is unable to monitor machine identities, enforce policies, or maintain effective management, all of which create significant risks.

The most common audit findings include an incomplete inventory of machine identities, the use of unauthorized CAs, expired certificates, and unrestricted use of self-signed certificates. Auditors may also flag specific machine identity weaknesses, such as long lifetimes or weak key algorithms (we cover this in Chapter 4). If you're tasked with addressing these negative compliance findings and you don't have a machine identity protection program in place, you face a lengthy, manual project.

Consequences of Machine Identity Risks

When a machine identity is compromised and used in a cyber-attack or causes an outage, the negative consequences can be significant. And because the consequences of a breach or outage are interrelated, if you have a serious incident, you're likely to suffer from more than one repercussion:

>> **Damaged reputation:** Outages and breaches can wreak havoc on the reliability and availability of your services. The resulting erosion of customer and partner trust can damage your business's reputation and take months, or even years, to overcome.

>> **Loss of revenue:** Downtime from an outage or a breach can negatively impact your bottom line through the loss of critical services or the loss of customer and partner confidence.

>> **Costly remediation:** Slow incident response and inefficient machine identity operations make recovering from an unplanned outage, security event, or negative audit finding a lengthy and costly process. The longer it takes to fix the problem, the higher the risk of serious damage.

>> **Higher resource costs:** All machine identity risks require time and resources to mitigate them. And if you're relying on manual tasks to manage machine identities, these resource costs will increase dramatically.

>> **Loss of employment:** The cumulative impact of outages and attacks that use machine identities can be serious. Recently, several C-suite executives lost their jobs in the fallout from major breaches.

Chapter **3**

Looking at Why the Number of Machines is Exploding

The definition of *machine* is undergoing radical changes; it now includes a wide range of hardware and software — from smart machines and virtual servers to applications, algorithms, blockchain, and intelligent containers that run microservices. Organizations that were managing a few thousand machines a couple of years ago are now trying to manage hundreds of thousands or even millions of machines today. And these numbers are expected to grow by at least 25 percent per year.

As the number of machines in businesses increases, so does the number of corresponding machine identities. This exponential growth complicates the already complex challenge of maintaining effective, enterprise-wide machine identity protection. This chapter outlines the key trends driving the rising number of machines on enterprise networks.

Machine Identities in the Cloud

Cloud computing and virtualization have profoundly changed the definition of machines to include software that emulates physical servers. This shift in how IT networks are structured allows enterprises to run faster, improve network manageability, reduce maintenance, and quickly adjust resources to address fluctuations in business demand.

The widespread adoption of cloud infrastructure is spawning a tidal wave of virtual devices, which are created and destroyed with unprecedented speed. In many cases, machines are being built and changed by other machines at machine speed and scale. The speed and volume of these changes completely break traditional approaches to machine identity protection.

TECHNICAL STUFF

According to Datadog, a monitoring platform for cloud applications, the average life span of a virtual machine is just 23 days, compared with the expected three-to-five-year life span of a physical device. This means that the number of cloud machine identities that need to be issued and installed, and later decommissioned, is growing at an extraordinary rate.

The flexibility that makes cloud computing so valuable to businesses also makes securing communication to, from, and within the cloud much more complex. Without secure machine identities, it's simply not possible to keep cloud communication protected and private.

Machine Identities in DevOps

DevOps teams support innovation by compartmentalizing applications to accelerate deployment of incremental changes to small segments of software. This has ushered in an entirely new definition of machines — each individual container and module within an application requires a unique identity so it can communicate securely. The scale of the new containers and microservices required for DevOps increases the number of variables in the already complex task of securing machine-to-machine communications in the cloud.

TECHNICAL STUFF

According to Datadog, the average life span of a DevOps container is just 2.5 days; this is an order of magnitude shorter than virtual machines and hundreds of times shorter than the life span of physical devices. The increasing use of containerization to deploy fast, flexible applications is driving a massive increase in machine identities that need to be deployed and protected.

Machine Identities for Mobile

The number of mobile devices has outstripped the number of humans, and this trend shows no sign of slowing. The Radicati Group states that the number of mobile devices in use, including phones and tablets, will grow from over 11 billion in 2016 to over 16 billion in 2020.

Mobile devices have been around for a couple of decades, but the amount of enterprise data they store and process has increased substantially over the past few years. As a result, organizations need to uniquely identify and authenticate each mobile device connecting to their networks, as well as the various applications on these devices. If left unprotected, attackers can leverage a weak or vulnerable mobile machine identity to gain access to critical enterprise network services and assets and use them as part of a broader attack strategy.

How the IoT Adds to Machine Identities

When you think about the Internet of Things (IoT), you probably think about consumer products, such as smart home devices for remote control of lights, security cameras, and so on, or wearable devices such as activity trackers. However, the use of IoT devices in enterprises is growing just as fast.

From industrial machinery and intelligent transportation systems to health monitoring and emergency notification systems, a broad range of IoT devices is already being deployed by enterprises. And each of these devices requires network connectivity so it can collect and transfer data. As a result, the volume of IoT communications is expected to explode over the next five years.

WARNING

Because IoT devices typically have limited CPU and storage capabilities, the captured data must be transmitted to a central location where it can be collected, stored, and analyzed. Unless communications between IoT devices and extended enterprise networks are authenticated and protected with valid, unique machine identities, the data flowing from these devices can be stolen or compromised.

Expanding Use of Blockchain

Most people think of blockchain as the technology behind crypto currencies like Bitcoin, but the underlying technology is versatile. Blockchain is a decentralized database, or *distributed ledger*, of transactions in which the records, or blocks, are continually growing and being reconciled. Blockchain is used in financial transactions, stock trading, real estate transactions, supply chain operations, legal contracts, and other applications that need to accurately validate transactions across simultaneous updates.

Machine identities are a critical aspect of every blockchain implementation. Private keys are used to uniquely and securely identify the participants in each transaction. As the use of blockchains increases, the number of blockchain-related machine identities will increase dramatically. And because blockchain transactions are legally binding, and often irreversible, the security and protection of the machine identities connected with them are crucial.

The Growing Role of Smart Machines

The exponential increase in available processing power, storage capacity, and communication bandwidth is making it possible for many critical tasks to be outsourced to smart machines. Because smart machines can solve increasingly complex problems and make decisions automatically without human intervention, this technology is profoundly changing the way work is done.

Smart machines leverage artificial intelligence and machine learning. Their use in enterprises includes automated stock trading algorithms; robots; virtual personal assistants; unmanned aerial vehicles (UAVs), such as commercial drones; and self-driving cars.

Securing smart machine identities is increasingly important because smart machines are often connected to critical infrastructure. Cybercriminals who gain access to smart machine identities can greatly change the outcome of automated tasks outsourced to smart machines.

Chapter **4**

Facing Machine Identity Protection Challenges

Given the rapid rise in the number of new machines on enterprise networks, it's surprising that they're not better protected. Even in organizations that take cybersecurity seriously, the challenges inherent in traditional approaches to machine identity protection make it difficult to implement and maintain.

In this chapter, you discover the challenges that organizations face in providing effective machine identity protection, and you look at the key reasons most security programs fall short in this crucial area.

Organizational Challenges

Even though machine identities play a critical role in securing automated machine-to-machine communication, they're one of the least understood and weakly defended parts of companies' networks.

Dispersed responsibility

One of the biggest challenges in machine identity protection programs is overcoming the way enterprises assign responsibility for the management and security of machine identities. In an ideal situation, your security team would provide services that deliver policy-enforced, secure, and reliable key and certificate management. You would then require the different lines of business to rely on these services to minimize risk and comply with policy on the machines they control. However, what often happens is that each group that generates, uses, and maintains machine identities is left to determine how best to manage and protect them.

Because machines support so many different critical functions, numerous business units need machine identities. This results in teams with different goals and skills deciding how they'll secure the machine identities they control. And because many administrators don't fully understand the impact of machine identity protection, they often treat it as an afterthought. This comparative lack of attention routinely leaves machine identities untracked, unmanaged, unmonitored, and unsecured.

To put machine identity protection into perspective, can you imagine what would happen to your organization's security if you allowed each business unit to decide how to protect usernames and passwords? Securing machine-to-machine communications is equally as important, requiring consistently enforced key and certificate security.

Direct access to private keys

Private keys must be kept secret, and most of those used in machine identities are stored in files, often called *keystores*. The management and protection of these files and the keys they store is usually left to individual system administrators. This flexibility gives administrators direct access to the private keys when they need them, but it can also open the door to many actions that weaken overall security, such as making copies of private keys.

WARNING

Giving system administrators direct access to private keys becomes particularly problematic when an administrator is reassigned or terminated. You should revoke and replace the keys (machine identities) controlled by previous administrators. Then they can't be used by the ex-employee or anyone else — *but* most organizations skip this important security task because they can't track keys in relation to administrative reassignments or terminations.

On the other hand, most organizations immediately revoke usernames and passwords, especially those that provide privileged access, within minutes after any employee leaves the company.

Often, a former administrator still has access to keys simply because no one thought to revoke them. In this case, there are no malicious actions, but the keys are still vulnerable to compromise and misuse. A less innocent reason could be that the administrator keeps the keys because the employee wants continued access after leaving the company. Either way, unrestricted access to keys that should've been revoked can leave an organization exposed to substantial security risks.

As bad as these problems are, SSH keys, which don't have expiration dates, can present an even greater risk. Because SSH keys are rarely changed, an unscrupulous administrator can use the keys for nefarious purposes for extended periods of time.

Even when administrators don't have malicious intent, their lack of knowledge about the security requirements for private keys can cause them to be careless. For example, it's fairly routine to see keys placed on USB drives or file shares where they can be compromised by cybercriminals.

No visibility

Because most organizations don't have a complete and accurate inventory of their machine identities, they don't have any way to understand exactly how their machine identities are being used. This lack of enterprise-wide visibility prevents you from detecting anomalous use of machine identities, which is an early indicator of a breach.

Also, with limited visibility and tracking, certificates can unexpectedly expire, triggering critical service outages (we discuss this topic in Chapter 2). If you don't have the information you need to manage the entire certificate life cycle and proactively identify impending expiration dates, you can't create dependable, proactive certificate renewal processes.

To make matters worse, a lack of visibility can make it nearly impossible for you to track certificate ownership. If an administrator who controls a machine identity resigns, is terminated, or is reassigned, certificate ownership is in limbo. When one of these orphaned certificates expires, you're left scrambling because you don't have enough information about the certificate to respond quickly.

Similarly, a lack of visibility into machine identities can restrict incident response following a security event. Often, your security teams won't have enough information to assess the role of machine identities in a breach. The time it takes to collect this information causes delays in the incident response process. And in the aftermath of a security event, most security teams don't think about the need to rotate keys and certificates to prevent further exposure.

WARNING

If you don't rotate keys after a breach, attackers with compromised keys and certificates will continue to have access to your network devices and services. Of course, your organization would never accept limited visibility and weak management of usernames and passwords, yet most organizations accept a lack of visibility into machine identities, which often control high levels of privileged access.

Lack of expertise

When your administrators need advice about machine identities they control, they don't have many experts that they can consult. Surprisingly, even in organizations with hundreds of thousands of machine identities, there are just a few encryption experts on staff who understand the intricacies of the machine identity life cycle. Even in the best circumstances, these experts can't manage all the machine identities used across your enterprise.

To add insult to injury, the tools your organization uses to manage machine identities usually require in-depth know-how. This leaves your average system administrator using Google to figure out what to do.

Ineffective Management Tools

Just a few years ago, the number of machine identities in your organization was just a fraction of what you need today. Plus, earlier machine identities didn't need to be updated or changed as often as they do now, and machine identities weren't targeted as frequently by cybercriminals. But that's all changed. New risks have made the need to manage and protect machine identities far more urgent, but most organizations are still relying on the management tools they used a decade ago. We cover the problems with these tools in this section.

Manual tracking

Despite the automation of many IT functions, more than half of organizations still use manual tracking methods to manage their machine identities. Like these organizations, you may have tried to build an inventory of keys and certificates on spreadsheets or by using shared Intranet databases. This approach may have been sufficient for a limited number of physical machines, but with the surging number of physical and virtual machines on enterprise networks, this manual approach isn't just error-prone; it's completely impractical.

If you're using a manual approach, you're probably tracking only a tiny fraction of the machine identities used for a subset of critical services. This leaves the majority of your machine identities, including those that support important business functions, unmanaged and unprotected.

Home-grown scripts

When organizations try to automate manual machine identity processes, they often start by using custom software scripts. These programs rarely collect all the information necessary to protect and maintain machine identities and rapidly become cumbersome and difficult to maintain. And when the script developer changes positions or leaves the company, you're left with a custom-built tool that's difficult or impossible to adjust or use.

Siloed management tools

Because manual tracking simply isn't feasible, a growing number of organizations are turning to siloed management tools, such as those provided by Certificate Authorities (CAs), to manage their certificates. Unfortunately, this approach also has severe limitations.

The information that siloed management tools delivers simply isn't enough to keep your machine identities protected. For example, CA dashboards only let you manage certificates issued by that particular CA. Because virtually all enterprises use more than one CA, each CA dashboard only provides management for a limited set of certificates. As a result, it's difficult to prioritize security risks across all certificates or efficiently deploy limited IT and security resources to address those risks.

In addition, these siloed tools don't contain information about where certificates are installed, and without this most basic information, it's nearly impossible to track down a certificate's location quickly. Relying exclusively on these tools also makes it difficult to identify weaknesses or detect vulnerabilities either in the certificates or on the servers where they're installed. And what if someone in your organization decides to get a free or low-cost certificate from a CA that isn't authorized by your organization's certificate issuance policies? (This happens more often than you might think.) You won't find this in the dashboards provided by authorized CAs.

Figure 4-1 shows data collected by TechValidate (TVID: 180-783-238) on enterprise use of ineffective certificate management tools before implementing a machine identity protection program. More than half of the companies used only manual tracking.

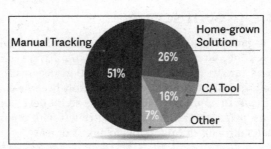

FIGURE 4-1: How companies manage machine identities.

Chapter **5**

Gathering Machine Identity Intelligence

Whether your organization is trying to prevent machine identity attacks or stop outages, there's a lot riding on the effectiveness of your machine identity protection program. But to create an effective program, you need technology specifically designed to address the unique management and security challenges of machine identities.

This chapter helps you identify the types of intelligence you need to collect so you can reduce security risks, eliminate outages, and consistently enforce a wide range of machine identity policies.

Getting Visibility Across All Your Machine Identities

Before you even begin a machine identity protection program, you need an inventory of all the machine identities used across your enterprise. To successfully gather this information, keep in mind the dynamic nature of machine identities and the different types of data necessary to protect them.

To build a successful machine identity protection program, you need these types of visibility:

>> **Extensive, enterprise-wide discovery:** First and foremost, you need a comprehensive, up-to-date view of all your machine identities, including those on virtual, cloud, mobile, and IoT infrastructures. While you can discover server certificates via port scanning, you must also be able to locate client and trusted Certificate Authority (CA) certificates, which require discovery of files and/or configuration data. Ideally, your inventory should include partner, supplier, and customer machine identities to ensure that setting up encrypted communication with them is safe.

>> **Central repository:** Any solution you implement should include a secure, central repository of machine identities to enable centralized access and comprehensive analysis.

>> **Broad machine identity support:** Look for a system that allows you to store data for various types of certificates and keys (for example, those for Secure Shell [SSH] and Transport Layer Security [TLS]) so you have an all-inclusive view across your machine identity assets.

>> **Reporting and analytics:** Equip your security analysts and stakeholders with the information they need to rapidly identify machine identity anomalies and vulnerabilities through dashboards, reports, analytics, and alerts tailored to their roles and areas of expertise.

Collecting Critical Types of Machine Identity Intelligence

To gain the intelligence you need to enforce policies and detect machine identity anomalies and vulnerabilities, you need to be able to discover and collect information on the critical attributes of each of your machine identities:

>> **Machine identity type:** To understand exactly how your machine identities are being used, you need to know the type of machine identity employed. Identifying whether machine identities are based on raw public keys (such as

SSH) or certificates is a critical first step. For certificates, identify whether they contain usage flags for server, client, code signing, email encryption, and so on — each of these instances has different risk profiles. Without this information, you won't be able to understand if a machine identity is being used inappropriately and, potentially, maliciously.

>> **Key strength:** Key length impacts key strength; the longer the key length, the more secure the key. Cybercriminals use *brute force* attacks that essentially try each possible key combination until they find one that can decrypt the data. So the shorter the key length, the easier it is for attackers to figure out the value of a private key.

REMEMBER

As more computational power becomes available to conduct brute force attacks, key strength requirements must evolve. Key lengths that are sufficient today may not be sufficient next month or year. You need information about key strength in order to find and replace weak keys and to provide evidence of compliance.

>> **Cryptographic algorithms:** Asymmetric algorithms, such as Rivest-Shamir-Adleman (RSA), Digital Signature Algorithm (DSA), and Elliptical Curve Digital Signature Algorithm (ECDSA), serve as the foundation for machine identities. Advances in quantum computing make it imperative that you monitor the use of asymmetric algorithms. This information helps you rapidly assess the level of risk from new cryptographic threats and vulnerabilities.

>> **Hash algorithms:** Weak hash algorithms on certificates make it more likely that attackers will be able to forge CA signatures and create rogue certificates that can be used to impersonate legitimate systems. For example, attackers successfully exploited weaknesses in the MD5 hash algorithm to spread malware by using the Windows update system through forged Microsoft certificates. More recently, successful collision attacks have been demonstrated on the SHA-1 hash algorithm.

>> **Length of validity:** Because most private keys are stored in files on the systems that they identify, the longer their validity period, the more likely they can be used to compromise those systems.

For example, if you don't revoke access to an administrator's private keys when the administrator is reassigned or terminated, the keys will remain active until the certificates expire, making short certificate life spans an important security criterion.

>> **Issuing CA:** Ensuring that your certificates are issued by approved CAs is fundamental to machine identity protection. You need to be able to find certificates issued by unauthorized CAs as well as self-signed certificates. Because these certificates don't follow policy or certificate management best practices and often go unmonitored, they increase your risk of security breaches and outages. Plus, they limit your ability to quickly replace large numbers of certificates in response to a security event.

This information provides a basic machine identity inventory that can be retrieved from the keys and certificates that serve as machine identities. However, to ensure that you can secure and protect your machine identities, you also need access to additional intelligence beyond what you can retrieve from the keys and certificates themselves:

>> **Location:** Up-to-date information about every machine where a key or certificate is installed is essential to the effective management of machine identities and is critical for incident response. Without location information, machine identity problems can be extremely difficult to diagnose and even harder to fix. Location information should include the machine address, file location, Hardware Security Module (HSM), if applicable, and account (for SSH keys, for example).

>> **Owner:** Machine identities exist across countless systems and different groups. Central public key infrastructure (PKI) and security teams rarely have the permissions necessary to manage these systems directly, and updates to machine identities often have to be performed locally. So, when a security vulnerability is detected, such as a weak algorithm, operational risk, or impending expiration, the PKI or security team needs to be able to rapidly contact the appropriate owner to solve the problem. On a broader scale, if a CA compromise occurs, the PKI or security team must immediately notify the owners of every system using certificates issued by that CA before replacement can begin.

>> **Cipher strength:** Each machine that uses a machine identity is configured to use certain ciphers, such as Advanced

Encryption Standard (AES). Weak ciphers undermine the strength of encryption and can facilitate compromises by cybercriminals.

>> **Protocol versions:** New vulnerabilities are regularly found in protocols like SSH and TLS. To reduce the chance of compromise, ensure that you're using only approved protocol versions.

>> **Certificate life cycle:** When you have complete visibility across the entire certificate life cycle, including length of validity and expiration dates, you can set policies to issue renewal notifications to certificate owners before certificates expire. This intelligence can also help set policies that ensure orphaned or unsecure machine identities are rotated out of use at specified intervals.

>> **Configuration:** Misconfigured servers, applications, or keystores may leave otherwise secure keys and certificates open to compromise. For SSH, configuration information can include source restrictions, force commands, whether port forwarding is allowed, and other security-critical requirements.

>> **Reputation scores:** The relative security of machine identities relies on multiple variables, and because there are so many rapid changes to machine identities, assessing risks quickly can be difficult. Reputation scores combine multiple machine identity attributes into a single numeric value that quickly indicates the risk associated with a specific certificate.

After you've gathered intelligence for all machine identities inside and outside your enterprise, you can use it to identify machine identity vulnerabilities, anomalies, risks, and trends. When dealing with tens of thousands — or even millions — of machine identities, automated analytics, dashboards, reporting, and alerts are the only way to rapidly identify risks across both broad and specific machine populations. As part of these automated processes, analytics should be sent to security information and event management (SIEM) and ticketing systems, and email alerts should be issued.

To highlight risks, reports must be able to collate critical data and translate it into actionable intelligence, and you need the flexibility to design specific reports for different audiences and deliver them on a regular schedule or on demand.

TIP

Machines and their machine identities support nearly every important business function. Business groups need machine identity intelligence for the systems they control so they can support security best practices and take rapid remedial action when needed.

Chapter **6**

Using Automation to Improve Machine Identity Protection

Afer you have access to comprehensive machine identity intelligence (which we cover in Chapter 5), you can identify machine identity vulnerabilities and risks. But if you attempt to address these risks and vulnerabilities by using manual methods, you can quickly become frustrated and overwhelmed. Automating your management and security processes is the most effective way to build and maintain a successful machine identity protection program.

In this chapter, we identify the different types of automation that are necessary to build machine identity protection. You explore how automation helps integrate machine identity intelligence with your technology ecosystem. We also show you how automating protection mitigates the risks we talk about in Chapter 2.

Bolstering Machine Identity Protection with Automation

Automation allows you to orchestrate a set of rapid actions that can be focused on a single machine identity or an entire group of identities at machine speed. These actions can be scheduled in advance, or they can be triggered by a specific set of conditions. To maximize the benefits of automation, you need five key capabilities.

Life cycle automation

Using manual processes to deploy, install, rotate, and replace machine identities is inherently error-prone and resource intensive. You will probably find it difficult to manually track the progress of complex, multi-step processes across multiple systems. Another shortcoming of manual management is that it gives your administrators direct access to private keys, which increases the possibility of private key compromise.

TECHNICAL STUFF

To manually deploy a new certificate, an administrator must generate a new key pair, generate a certificate signing request (CSR), submit the CSR to a Certificate Authority (CA), retrieve the issued certificate and CA certificate chain from the CA, install the certificate and CA chain, configure the application, and often restart the application. The certificate and private key may also need to be installed on multiple systems if you're using clustering or load balancing.

TIP

Automating the entire machine identity life cycle provides these benefits:

>> Ensures that all tasks are performed consistently across the enterprise, no matter how many machine identities or how many different uses of these machine identities are employed in your organization — this includes managing certificate requests, issuance, installation, validation, renewals, and replacements

>> Decommissions machine identities quickly to prevent unused machine identities from being exploited by cybercriminals

>> Improves security by removing administrator access to keystores

» Simplifies the adoption of Hardware Security Modules (HSMs) to improve the protection of private keys on mission-critical systems

Policy enforcement

Automation is a critical capability that makes it possible to consistently enforce your organization's corporate machine identity policies and applicable regulatory requirements. When you leave compliance in the hands of the various administrators who manage keys and certificates for the systems they control, the policy enforcement results will be inconsistent.

For the best results, automated policy enforcement should drive every aspect of your machine identities, including configuration, issuance, use, ownership, management, security, and decommissioning. With these capabilities, you can automatically revoke and replace any machine identities that don't conform to appropriate policies. Plus, you'll have the flexibility to enforce machine identity policies in a variety of ways: globally, by logical group, or by individual identity.

TIP

One way security teams can leverage automation to deliver secure machine identities is to build a self-service portal. This approach allows your system administrators to easily manage the machine identities they control. And because security policies are automatically applied to machine identities issued through the portal, your security team will know that corporate policies and industry regulations are being enforced.

Remediation

Automation also gives you the agility you need to rapidly respond to critical security events such as a CA compromise or zero-day vulnerability in a cryptographic algorithm or library. For example, if a large-scale security event occurs, automation is the only way you can quickly make bulk changes to all affected certificates, private keys, and CA certificate chains. Automation is also the fastest way to remediate more focused security events, such as replacing a compromised certificate that's used across multiple machines.

Validation

Because machine identities include a complex set of variables, determining whether they're properly installed and configured is difficult if you're using manual installation. Validating the installation and proper use of machine identities is complicated because they're stored and used across a diverse range of devices, applications, and containers. But without access to this information, you won't be able to tell whether any configuration changes you make will impact the security and operation of your machine identities.

Automation can solve these problems by validating that every machine identity is installed properly and working correctly. Ongoing validation ensures that your machine identities continue to be effectively managed and secured. Validation is also useful when you're grappling with large-scale security events. For example, when responding to a CA compromise or vulnerable algorithm, you need to have an accurate assessment of the progress of machine identity replacement across the enterprise.

Continuous monitoring

Machine identity intelligence loses its value if it only represents a single point in time. Automating your intelligence gathering is the only way to continually monitor the security and health of your machine identities. Plus, when your intelligence is automatically updated, you can generate alerts when anomalies or vulnerabilities are detected.

Without continuous monitoring, it's easy to miss several of the changes that are common to machine identities:

>> Rapid changes on cloud and virtual servers and the applications that run on them

>> Software update failures that cause configurations to be rolled back, overwriting a new certificate with an old, potentially vulnerable or expired certificate

>> The deployment and use of certificates from an unauthorized CA

>> Insecure DevOps test certificates that are inadvertently rolled out to production

These examples are just a few of the millions of changes to machine identities that are happening constantly, but they illustrate why you need comprehensive, continuous monitoring for every machine identity used in your organization.

TIP

When you've set up your machine identity protection program to continually capture the information you need, you can rely on that intelligence to drive automated actions. The more management and security processes that can be reliably automated, the more benefits you see — from fewer errors to a reduction in management resources and better security.

Integrating with Your Technology Ecosystem

Machine identities are used by nearly all the technology solutions that are deployed across your expanded network and security infrastructure. You need to be prepared to integrate and orchestrate machine identities across a multitude of enterprise IT systems.

Operating systems and applications

Enterprises rely on a broad range of operating systems (AIX, Red Hat, Solaris, Windows, and so on) and applications (Apache, Web-Sphere, IIS, and more) for their mission-critical operations. Each of these systems and applications has a machine identity that plays a fundamental role in the security of communications to and from these systems.

Access to machine identity intelligence allows you to automate key and CSR generation for certificates and CA certificate chain installation, validation, and renewal. Automating access to machine identities helps to preserve the uptime and security of these important systems, and it's the most efficient way to encrypt both internal and external traffic.

Load balancing

Load balancers have become a primary conduit through which organizations manage and process communications with customers, partners, and employees. Because load balancers front end so many applications, they also host a large number of machine identities that represent each backend application. Due to the critical nature of the services load balancers handle and the scale of machine identities they host — sometimes more than 1,000 machine identities per load balancer — you can't easily collect intelligence or manage the life cycle of these machine identities without automation.

TLS inspection

Transport Layer Security (TLS) inspection devices provide critical visibility into TLS data streams. To do this, they must have access to the private keys for the thousands of systems on which they are monitoring traffic. To support TLS inspection at this scale, you need the ability to automatically and securely transfer and install private keys on TLS inspection devices.

Hardware security modules

Most private keys are stored in files on the systems they secure. This makes them susceptible to compromise. To prevent these risks, you can use HSM solutions to generate, store, and access keys within the safe confines of a security-hardened appliance. Using HSMs also helps you simplify compliance because auditors understand their security benefits.

However, adding HSMs can also increase management complexity because they add a layer between your systems and your private keys. You can avoid this complexity by integrating machine identity automation into your HSM processes.

Cloud and DevOps platforms

Cloud and DevOps platforms require the rapid creation and provisioning of machine identities to ensure secure computing and application deployment. If you automate the delivery and monitoring of machine identities in each of these environments, you can increase security while supporting the deployment of new servers, applications, and containers at machine speed.

Security information and event management

Integrating automated machine identity intelligence directly into Security Information and Event Management (SIEM) platforms allows your security teams to correlate machine identity intelligence with other security information. This correlation helps accelerate the identification and remediation of cyber threats.

Other enterprise systems and services

In addition to the systems outlined in this chapter, you also need the ability to integrate machine identity security and protection with other enterprise systems, such as identity management solutions, configuration management databases, ticketing systems, and change control. With these integrations, you can streamline operations and improve security.

Overcoming Machine Identity Risks with Automation

In Chapter 2, we outline the risks of weak machine identity protection. Intelligence–driven automation is the only approach that can address these, and many other, machine identity risks. To help avoid the impacts of these risks, follow these guidelines:

>> **Avoid certificate-related outages** by eliminating manual errors and automating the entire certificate life cycle to ensure machine identities are renewed before they expire. Information on certificate location and ownership quickly targets renewal requests with automated escalations as needed.

>> **Prevent breaches** by automating the collection of risk intelligence required to quickly identify and respond to machine identity vulnerabilities, weaknesses, or security events. Automated policy-enforcement and life cycle management ensure unused or old keys and certificates are decommissioned.

>> **Accelerate incident response** by automating the identification of impacted keys and certificates as well as the actions needed to remediate large groups of machine identities, so you can dramatically increase the speed of your response to large-scale security events.

>> **Streamline operations** by automating routine administrative tasks to eliminate manual, error-prone processes and reduce the expertise and resources needed to protect the growing number of machine identities.

>> **Ensure compliance** by automating policy enforcement to improve audit readiness, offering automated validation of machine identity protection, and generating scheduled or on-demand compliance reports.

REMEMBER

Automation also makes it easy to implement role-based access controls that allow or block access to machine identities. Implementing change management and role-based access controls ensures you can effectively manage machine identities and demonstrate this control for audits.

Figure 6-1 shows data collected by TechValidate (TVID:BD2-B96-089) on how organizations with a machine identity protection program are using automation to overcome risks and reduce machine identity protection challenges.

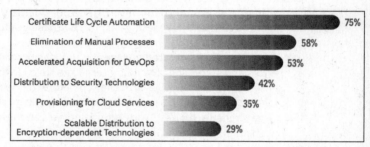

Certificate Life Cycle Automation — 75%
Elimination of Manual Processes — 58%
Accelerated Acquisition for DevOps — 53%
Distribution to Security Technologies — 42%
Provisioning for Cloud Services — 35%
Scalable Distribution to Encryption-dependent Technologies — 29%

FIGURE 6-1: How companies are using automation in machine identity protection programs.

Chapter 7

Ten Steps to Machine Identity Protection

Secure communications between machines are essential to the success of every enterprise. But how do you keep the identities of your machines safe when machines are added and changed every day? To build your own machine identity protection program, you need to take specific steps. We cover that process in this chapter, and together these steps enable your organization to protect all the machine identities you're using today and positions you to keep up with the growing number of machines your enterprise will need moving forward.

Here are the steps to follow:

1. **Locate all your machine identities.**

Getting a list of all your machine identities and knowing where they're all installed, who owns them, and how they're used is the first step in protecting them. After your discovery is complete, you'll have visibility into your keys, certificates, and the machines on which they're installed as well as the rest of the metadata that makes up machine identities. This information is used to communicate trustworthiness, provide encryption, and protect machine-to-machine communication.

2. **Set up and enforce security policies.**

   To keep your machine identities safe, you need to set up corporate policies and best practices to govern these critical security assets. This helps you control every aspect of machine identities — issuance, use, ownership, management, security, and decommissioning. Enforcing policies also ensures that your machine identities comply with industry and government regulations.

REMEMBER

   Defining certificate policies is important, but those policies won't improve security or compliance if you can't enforce them. Automating the enforcement of machine identity policies ensures that you're maximizing the security of every machine identity your organization uses.

3. **Continuously gather machine identity intelligence.**

   Because the number and type of machines on your network are constantly changing, you need an ongoing program to update intelligence on your machine identities. Some of this intelligence is available within the machine identity itself, and some you need to gather from the conditions of its use and its environment. This information is critical to your ability to drive intelligent, automated actions in your machine identity protection program.

4. **Automate the machine identity life cycle.**

   It's important that you automate the entire machine identity life cycle, including the management of certificate requests, issuance, installation, renewals, and replacements. Automating the life cycle allows you to avoid error-prone, resource-intensive manual actions, while improving operations and security.

WARNING

   If you can't automate your machine identity life cycle, you will increase the risk of experiencing certificate-related outages and serious security breaches.

5. **Validate correct installation and configuration.**

   Validation ensures that machine identities are installed properly and working correctly. Validation not only helps you with ongoing management and security, it also demonstrates compliance and shows progress when you need to replace a large number of machine identities.

6. **Monitor for anomalous use.**

After you've established a baseline of normal machine identity usage, you can start monitoring and flagging anomalous behavior, which can indicate a machine identity compromise.

7. **Set up notifications and alerts.**

The ability to find and evaluate potential machine identity issues before they become business interruptions or exposures is critical. If you set up automated alerts and notifications based on policy, they can inform you of unauthorized changes or impending actions that need to be taken. Automated alerts allow you to take immediate action before outages happen or attackers take advantage of weak or unprotected machine identities.

8. **Remediate machine identities that don't conform to policy.**

After a policy change, continuous monitoring can flag if the change results in another policy being violated or otherwise causes a machine identity to be noncompliant. When this happens, you must act quickly. Automated, intelligence-driven action allows you to quickly address all compliance issues as well as quickly respond to any security incident that requires bulk remediation.

9. **Use a self-service portal to provide easy access to machine identities.**

Providing end-users with an easy way to access machine identities allows you to quickly deliver secure, policy-enforced machine identities to all business units. Plus, integrating self-service solutions with DevOps and cloud platforms allows your developers to seamlessly request and install certificates without incurring any delays.

10. **Integrate with your technology ecosystem.**

You can improve the effectiveness of your network and security systems by integrating machine identity management and security, giving these crucial technologies easy access to up-to-date keys and certificates and machine identity intelligence.

Notes

Notes

Notes

Notes